tomatoes

Great recipe ideas with a classic ingredient

>> in 60 ways

Marshall Cavendish
Cuisine

Editor: Sylvy Soh
Designer: Lynn Chin Nyuk Ling
Photography: Joshua Tan, Elements By The Box

Copyright © 2008 Marshall Cavendish International (Asia) Private Limited

Published by Marshall Cavendish Cuisine
An imprint of Marshall Cavendish International
1 New Industrial Road, Singapore 536196

Other Marshall Cavendish Offices:
Marshall Cavendish Ltd. 5th Floor, 32-38 Saffron Hill, London EC1N 8FH,
UK · Marshall Cavendish Corporation. 99 White Plains Road, Tarrytown
NY 10591-9001, USA · Marshall Cavendish International (Thailand) Co Ltd.
253 Asoke, 12th Flr, Sukhumvit 21 Road, Klongtoey Nua, Wattana, Bangkok
10110, Thailand · Marshall Cavendish (Malaysia) Sdn Bhd, Times Subang,
Lot 46, Subang Hi-Tech Industrial Park, Batu Tiga, 40000 Shah Alam,
Selangor Darul Ehsan, Malaysia

Marshall Cavendish is a trademark of Times Publishing Limited

National Library Board Singapore Cataloguing in Publication Data

Tomatoes in 60 ways : great recipe ideas with a classic ingredient -
Singapore: Marshall Cavendish Cuisine, 2008.
p. cm.
ISBN-13 : 978-981-261-535-0
ISBN-10 : 981-261-535-0

1. Cookery (Tomatoes) I. Title: Tomatoes in sixty ways

TX803.T6
641.65642 -- dc22   OCN191781091

Printed in Singapore by Times Graphics Pte Ltd

contents »

introduction >>

Although they are regarded and consumed as vegetables, tomatoes are botanically classified as a fruit. Whether sliced for a simple salad, diced to make a tasty salsa dip or juiced for drinking, tomatoes have established themselves as an essential ingredient in cooking. Their unique, juicy sweetness is unrivalled, and they maintain versatility when used as a main or supporting ingredient.

Tomatoes were first cultivated in south America. They were introduced to the rest of the world after Spanish colonisation of the Americas, when the Spanish introduced tomato seeds to their colonies such as the Caribbean and the Philippines. Eventually, they also made their way to Europe and North America between the 16th and 17th centuries. As it is a member of the nightshade family, which includes plants with a toxin, the tomato was initially an unpopular crop. Tomato plants were thus primarily cultivated for ornamental purposes in Europe, but they eventually made their way to North America, where they gained acceptance as a food.

Tomatoes are now cultivated and consumed throughout the world. In France, they form an integral part of the classic vegetable casserole, ratatouille. The Greeks and Italians enjoy them in pastas and pizzas and also eat them raw, drizzled with a simple combination of olive oil and fresh herbs. In India, tomatoes are puréed and incorporated into creamy curries or used to flavour rice. The Chinese make use of their sweet, tart flavour to make a piquant sweet and sour sauce for stir-fried meat dishes.

For those who have difficulty envisioning tomatoes to be anything beyond the generic slice of vegetable found in sandwiches, or bottled ketchup, this book will bring out the tomato's true potential.

Varieties

Globe, cherry and plum (Roma) tomatoes are varieties that are commonly available. Globe tomatoes have a mild flavour and are good for grilling and slicing. Cherry tomatoes tend to be sweet and juicy, and are commonly used for salads, or eaten raw as a snack. Plum (Roma) tomatoes have relatively fewer seeds as compared to other varieties, which make them an ideal choice for canning or making sauces and purées.

Nutritional Content

Like chillies and capsicums (bell peppers), tomatoes contain a high amount of vitamin C, as well as vitamins A and K. They also contain lycopene, a carotenoid that has antioxidant and cancer-fighting properties.

Choosing and Storing Tomatoes

Choose firm tomatoes that are glossy and unblemished, with a taut skin. When possible, choose vine-ripened tomatoes, as they have a better flavour compared to those that are artificially ripened off the vine. Unripe tomatoes can be placed in a paper bag with bananas to speed up the ripening process.

Tomatoes should be stored away from direct sunlight and at room temperature. If possible, do not store them in the refrigerator, as the cold affects their flavour. If refrigerating, store them in the vegetable drawer of the refrigerator. Leave refrigerated tomatoes to stand at room temperature for at least 30 minutes before use so they may regain their flavour.

soups & beverages

minestrone

Fuss-free and convenient, this filling and nutritious soup can be prepared in the microwave oven in a matter of minutes, and is great especially if one is rushed for time.

Serves 4

Ingredients

Streaky bacon	100 g ($3\frac{1}{2}$ oz), trimmed and chopped
Celery	1 stalk
Carrots	2, peeled and diced
Onions	2, peeled and chopped
Garlic	1 clove, peeled and crushed
Butter	1 Tbsp
Chopped fresh basil	1 tsp, or $\frac{1}{2}$ tsp dried basil
Canned chopped tomatoes	1 can, about 390 g (14 oz)
Vegetable or chicken stock	850 ml (28 fl oz / $3\frac{1}{2}$ cups)
Canned cannellini beans	200 g (7 oz), rinsed and drained
Green cabbage	55 g (2 oz), shredded
Long-grain rice	55 g (2 oz)
Italian meat sausage	55 g (2 oz), cut into small cubes
Chopped fresh parsley	2 Tbsp
Salt	to taste
Ground white pepper	to taste

Method

• Place bacon in a large microwave-safe bowl. Cover and cook in the microwave oven on High for 2 minutes. Add celery, carrots, onions, garlic, butter and basil and stir to mix well. Cover and return to the microwave oven on High for another 10 minutes, stirring twice.

• Add tomatoes and 625 ml (20 fl oz / $2\frac{1}{2}$ cups) stock. Stir to mix well, cover and cook in the microwave oven on High for 8 minutes, stirring once.

• Add beans, cabbage, rice, sausage, remaining stock, parsley, salt and pepper. Stir to mix well. Cover and cook in the microwave oven on High for 10–12 minutes, or until the vegetables and rice are tender, stirring once or twice.

• Dish out and serve hot.

NOTE

Minestrone can also be cooked over the stove using a medium-size heavy saucepan. Maintain medium heat throughout cooking.

red gazpacho

Gazpacho is a cold soup that originates from the southern region of Andalusia, Spain. This version has its ingredients puréed in a blender and is the perfect starter for meals on hot summer days.

Serves 4

Ingredients

Ripe tomatoes	450 g (1 lb)
Cucumber	1/2, peeled and roughly chopped
Red capsicum (bell pepper)	1, cored, seeded and roughly chopped
Spanish onion	1/2, peeled and roughly chopped
Garlic	3 cloves, peeled and roughly chopped
Baguette (French loaf)	1 small loaf, crusts removed
Vegetable stock	435 ml (14 fl oz / 1 3/4 cups)
Wine vinegar	1 Tbsp
Olive oil	2 Tbsp
Tomato purée	3 Tbsp
Salt	to taste
Ground black pepper	to taste

Croutons

Sliced white bread	4
Olive oil	1 Tbsp

Method

- Cut a small 'x' at the bottom of each tomato. Bring a pot of water to the boil and place tomatoes in for 30 seconds. Remove and plunge them immediately into cold water for another 30 seconds, then remove and drain. Peel and discard skins. Cut tomatoes into quarter, then scoop out and discard soft centres.

- In a blender, combine tomatoes, cucumber, capsicum, onion, garlic and baguette and blend for 30 seconds or until smooth. Do this in batches if necessary.

- With the motor still running, gradually add stock, vinegar, oil and tomato purée. Blend well and season to taste with salt and pepper. Transfer to a container, cover and refrigerate for at least 2 hours.

- Meanwhile, prepare croutons. Remove crusts from sliced bread, then cut into 1.5-cm (3/4-in) cubes. In a pan, heat olive oil and fry bread cubes for 5 minutes, or until crisp and golden. Remove from heat and drain on absorbent paper.

- Ladle gazpacho into 4 serving bowls and garnish as desired. Serve with croutons on the side.

tomato soup

The fresh taste of tomatoes are prevalent in this simple but delicious soup . Serve with warm crusty bread or with lightly toasted rounds of French bread spread thickly with cream cheese for a dinner party.

Serves 4

Ingredients

Butter	2 Tbsp
Tomatoes	700 g (1$\frac{1}{2}$ lb)
Chicken stock	1 litre (32 fl oz / 4 cups)
Onion	1, medium, peeled and finely chopped
Bay leaf	1
Orange	1, grated for 2 tsp zest
Salt	$\frac{1}{4}$ tsp
Ground black pepper	$\frac{1}{2}$ tsp
Lemon juice	2 tsp
Sugar	1 tsp

Method

• In a medium saucepan, melt butter over low heat. When foam subsides, add tomatoes and cook for 10 minutes, stirring continuously. Increase to medium heat and add stock, onion, bay leaf and orange zest. Season with salt and pepper and return mixture to the boil.

• Reduce heat to low and leave mixture to simmer for 45 minutes, stirring occasionally to prevent burning. Remove from heat and strain mixture into another saucepan. Using the back of a wooden spoon, press tomato pulp through strainer until only dry pulp is left. Discard dry pulp.

• Heat strained mixture over low heat, add lemon juice and sugar and bring to the boil for 5 minutes, stirring to mix well. Garnish as desired and serve immediately.

tomato & courgette soup

Lightly spiced with nutmeg, this creamy, filling soup is a meal in itself. Serve with warm crusty bread.

Serves 6

Ingredients

Ripe tomatoes	900 g (2 lb)
Chicken stock	2 litres (64 fl oz / 8 cups)
Courgettes (zucchinis)	6, trimmed, blanched and chopped
Butter	55 g (2 oz)
Plain (all-purpose) flour	30 g (1 oz)
Salt	1 tsp
Ground black pepper	1 tsp
Grated nutmeg	1 tsp
Sugar	2 tsp
Finely chopped fresh parsley	1 Tbsp
Finely chopped fresh dill	1 Tbsp
Sour cream	125 ml (4 fl oz / $\frac{1}{2}$ cup)

Method

- Cut a small 'x' at the bottom of each tomato. Bring a pot of water to the boil and place tomatoes in for 30 seconds. Remove and plunge them immediately into cold water for another 30 seconds, then remove and drain. Peel and discard skins. Cut tomatoes into quarters, then scoop out and discard soft centres.

- In a large, heavy-based saucepan, pour in half of chicken stock and add tomatoes and courgettes and bring to the boil over high heat, stirring continuously. Reduce heat to low and leave mixture to simmer for 15–20 minutes, until courgettes are soft.

- Meanwhile, melt butter in a small saucepan over medium heat. When foam subsides, remove from heat and stir in flour with a wooden spoon until a smooth paste is formed. Add 4 Tbsp soup and stir to blend well. Return mixture to saucepan with soup and cook for 2–3 minutes, stirring continuously or until smooth and thickened.

- Gradually add remaining stock and return mixture to the boil. Add salt, pepper, nutmeg, sugar, parsley and dill and stir to mix well.

- Remove from heat and stir in sour cream. Dish out and serve immediately.

tomato lassi

This North Indian beverage makes a refreshing drink for hot days.

Serves 1

Ingredients

Salt	a pinch
Cold water	125 ml (4 fl oz / $\frac{1}{2}$ cup)
Tomato juice	4 Tbsp, chilled
Plain yoghurt	4 Tbsp, chilled
Celery salt	$\frac{1}{4}$ tsp
Crushed ice	

Method

- In a blender, combine all ingredients except crushed ice blend well. Half-fill a tall glass with crushed ice and pour mixture over. Serve immediately.

iced tomato vodka

An aperitif and starter all in one, this drink will get your party off to a flying start! Start preparations for this about 6 hours ahead.

Serves 6

Ingredients

Tomato juice	300 ml (10 fl oz / 1$\frac{1}{4}$ cups)
Vodka	85 ml (2$\frac{1}{2}$ fl oz / $\frac{1}{3}$ cup)
Lemons	2, squeezed for juice
Worchestershire sauce	4–6 drops
Ice cubes	6, crushed
Green capsicum (bell pepper)	$\frac{1}{2}$, cored, seeded and finely diced
Celery leaves	4, chopped
Celery salt	to taste
Salt	to taste
Ground black pepper	to taste

Garnish (optional)

Mint or watercress leaves

Method

- In a blender, pour in tomato juice, vodka, lemon juice, Worchestershire sauce and ice and blend at high speed for 1 minute or until ice is finely crushed. Add capsicum, celery leaves, celery salt and salt and pepper and pulse mixture until well blended.

- Pour mixture into a freezer tray and freeze for 1–2 hours. Scrape mixture with a fork to break up the crystals, then return to the freezer for another 2–3 hours until mixture is firm.

- Transfer mixture to the refrigerator to soften slightly 30 minutes before serving. Spoon into serving glasses and garnish with mint or watercress leaves if desired before serving.

snacks & appetisers

eggs in tomato shells

This Portuguese dish is usually served cold as a first course, or with a mixed greens salad as a light lunch.

Serves 6

Ingredients

Firm tomatoes	6, large
Salt	1 tsp
Ground black pepper	$1/2$ tsp
Olive oil	2 Tbsp
Onion	1, small, peeled and finely chopped
Chopped fresh basil	2 tsp, or $1/2$ tsp dried basil
Tomato purée	1 Tbsp
Hard-boiled eggs	6, peeled
Mayonnaise	4 Tbsp

Method

• Cut a small 'x' at the bottom of each tomato. Bring a pot of water to the boil and place tomatoes in for 30 seconds. Remove and plunge them immediately into cold water for another 30 seconds, then remove and drain. Peel and discard skins.

• Cut caps off tomatoes so there is an opening big enough to insert an egg. Carefully scoop out pulp and seeds and reserve caps, pulp and seeds. Sprinkle insides of tomato shells with $1/2$ tsp salt and $1/4$ tsp pepper. Set aside.

• In a small saucepan, heat oil over medium heat. Fry onion until soft and translucent. Add reserved tomato caps, pulp, seeds, basil, tomato purée and remaining salt and pepper. Stir to mix well, then reduce heat to low. Cover and simmer for 15–20 minutes or until sauce has thickened. Remove from heat and set aside to cool.

• Place tomato shells on a serving dish. Stuff an egg into each shell and refrigerate for 20 minutes to chill.

• Add mayonnaise to sauce and stir to mix well. Transfer to a small bowl and refrigerate to chill.

• Spoon sauce over eggs and garnish as desired. Serve immediately.

broiled tomatoes

Drizzled with olive oil, then sprinkled with garlic, dried oregano and Parmesan cheese, these broiled tomatoes can be quickly whipped up and served as an appetiser or side dish.

Serves 4–6

Ingredients

Tomatoes	4, cut into 0.5-cm (¼-in) slices
Olive oil	4 Tbsp
Garlic	2 cloves, peeled and minced
Dried oregano	1 tsp
Parmesan cheese	70 g (2½ oz)
Sea salt	to taste
Ground black pepper	to taste

Method

- Line a broiler tray with aluminium foil and arrange tomato slices in a single layer.
- Drizzle tomatoes lightly with olive oil, then sprinkle with garlic, oregano and Parmesan cheese. Season with salt and pepper to taste.
- Broil at 180°C (350°F) for 3–5 minutes, or until cheese is brown and melted.
- Transfer to a serving dish and serve immediately.

oven-roasted cherry tomato bruschetta

This classic Italian starter will make a great starter for a luncheon or party. Simply pop the tomatoes in the oven and forget about them until they're ready!

Makes 12

Ingredients

Red cherry tomatoes	350 g (12 oz)
Yellow cherry tomatoes	350 g (12 oz)
Extra virgin olive oil	1 Tbsp
Garlic	3 cloves, peeled and minced
Salt	$\frac{1}{2}$ tsp
Ground black pepper	$\frac{1}{2}$ tsp
Fresh basil leaves	a large handful, finely sliced into strips
Red wine vinegar	1 Tbsp
Baguettes (French loaves)	3, cut into 12 slices. each 10 x 1.5-cm (4 x $\frac{3}{4}$-in)

Method

- Preheat oven to 160°C (325°F).

- Combine tomatoes, oil, garlic, salt and pepper in a bowl. Toss to mix well, then place on a lined baking tray. Bake for 40–50 minutes, or until tomatoes are soft, with their juices running.

- In the last 10 minutes of baking, toast baguette slices until light golden brown and set aside.

- Place tomatoes in a mixing bowl and add basil and vinegar. Toss gently to mix well.

- Arrange baguette slices on a serving tray and spoon tomato mixture over. Serve immediately.

prawn and pork stuffed tomatoes

The intense red colour of these tomatoes filled with a juicy stuffing of minced pork and prawns makes a pretty contrast with the yellow egg nets.

Makes 10

Ingredients

Tomatoes	10
Salt	1 heaped tsp
Coriander leaves (cilantro)	a handful, finely chopped
Garlic	3 cloves, peeled and chopped
Black peppercorns	8
Lean minced pork	250 g (9 oz)
Prawns (shrimps)	300 g (11 oz), peeled and minced
Onion	1, peeled and chopped
Sugar	1 tsp
Fish sauce	2 Tbsp
Eggs	4, beaten

Method

• Slice caps off tomatoes and set aside to be used as lids. Scoop out pulp and seeds, then sprinkle insides of tomato shells with salt. Lay out a few sheets of kitchen paper, overturn tomatoes on top and leave aside to drain for 20 minutes.

• Using a mortar and pestle, pound coriander, garlic and peppercorns until fine. Place in a mixing bowl together with pork, prawns, onion, sugar, fish sauce and 1 egg. Mix well and set aside.

• Preheat oven to 180°C (350°F).

• Rinse and dry tomato shells. Spoon in prawn and pork mixture until tightly stuffed so that tomatoes retain their shape even after baking. Replace lids and place on a lined baking tray. Bake for 30 minutes.

• Meanwhile, lightly grease a frying pan with cooking oil and place over medium heat. Dip your fingers into remaining beaten egg and drizzle in a criss-cross pattern into pan until it resembles a net. Carefully lift egg net out and set aside. Repeat to make 9 more nets.

• Remove tomatoes from oven and wrap with egg nets. Serve immediately.

green tomato fritters

This is a classic southern American dish that is enjoyed as a snack. Serve with a fresh green salad on the side.

Serves 4–5

Ingredients

Green tomatoes	3, large
Corn meal	2 Tbsp
Baking powder	$^1/_2$ tsp
Salt	to taste
Ground black pepper	to taste
Egg	1, large, beaten
Cooking oil	

Method

- Cut tomatoes in half, scoop out pulp and seeds and chop into 0.5-cm ($^1/_4$-in) cubes.

- In a mixing bowl, combine corn meal, baking powder, salt and pepper. Add tomato cubes and egg and mix until batter is neither too runny nor thick. Adjust consistency by adding more corn meal or water as necessary.

- Lightly grease a frying pan with oil and place over medium-high heat. Make each fritter using 1 Tbsp batter, spacing them out so they do not run into each other. Fry 3–4 fritters at a time, depending on size of pan. Fry until batter is crisp and golden brown on both sides. Remove from heat and drain well on absorbent paper. Repeat until remaining batter is used up.

- Serve immediately.

tomato chutney

Sweet and savoury, this chutney goes well as a condiment for meat and poultry dishes and is also a tasty sandwich spread.

Makes about 6 lb (2.7 kg)

Ingredients

Ripe tomatoes	1.3 kg (2 lb 13 oz)
Green apples	1.3 kg (2 lb 13 oz), cored and diced
Onions	3, large, peeled and finely chopped
Sultanas	350 g (12 oz)
Raisins	350 g (12 oz)
Dry mustard	$1^1/_2$ tsp
Ground ginger	$1^1/_2$ tsp
Salt	1 Tbsp
Ground allspice	1 tsp
Soft brown sugar	700 g ($1^1/_2$ lb)
Malt vinegar	625 ml (20 fl oz / $2^1/_2$ cups)

Method

- Cut a small 'x' at the bottom of each tomato. Bring a pot of water to the boil and place tomatoes in for 30 seconds. Remove and plunge them immediately into cold water for another 30 seconds, then remove and drain. Peel and discard skins, then cut tomatoes into small chunks.

- Combine all ingredients and place in a large saucepan over high heat. Bring to the boil, then reduce to low heat and leave to simmer for 2 hours, stirring occasionally, or until chutney has thickened.

- Remove from heat and ladle chutney into clean, warmed jam jars. Place a circle of vinegar-proof paper over chutney and seal each jar with a jam cover and elastic band.

NOTE

Malt vinegar helps to preserve the chutney so that it will keep well even without refrigeration. If refrigerated, chutney will keep for a longer period of time. Take care to prevent chutney from coming into contact with water.

spinach-stuffed tomato flowers

In addition to being healthy and delicious, this simple dish is also aesthetically pleasing. Serve as a starter, or as part of a main meal.

Serves 6

Ingredients

Firm tomatoes	6, large
Vinaigrette	125 ml (4 fl oz / ½ cup)
Spinach	350 g (12 oz)
Lemon juice	1 tsp
Olive oil	1 tsp
Grated nutmeg	a pinch
Salt	to taste
Ground black pepper	to taste
Very finely chopped onion	3 Tbsp
Hard-boiled eggs	2, peeled and sliced

Method

• Place tomatoes stalk end down on a cutting board. Using a very sharp knife, cut each tomato into 6 wedge-shaped petals without cutting through the tomato completely. Open tomatoes very carefully and place in a small container. Pour vinaigrette over and leave to marinate for at least 2 hours.

• Wash and drain spinach leaves and discard any leaves and stems that are blemished. Place in a saucepan over high heat and cook for 2 minutes or until spinach wilts, stirring constantly.

• Drain spinach well, then lightly squeeze to remove moisture. Chop coarsely and mix with 3 Tbsp vinaigrette used to marinate tomatoes. Season with lemon juice, olive oil, nutmeg, salt and pepper. Refrigerate until ready to use.

• Drain tomatoes well. Spoon a mound of spinach into the centre of each tomato and garnish with chopped onion. Serve immediately with hard-boiled egg slices on the side.

tomato aspic

Tomato aspic may be served as a first course or as a salad. Alternatively, dice it and use as a garnish for cold egg, meat and fish dishes.

Serves 4

Ingredients

Chicken stock	300 ml (10 fl oz / 1$\frac{1}{4}$ cups), heated until hot
Tomato juice	375 ml (12 fl oz / 1$\frac{1}{2}$ cups)
Tomato purée	2 Tbsp
Sugar	$\frac{1}{2}$ tsp
Egg shell	1, cleaned and crushed
Egg white	1, lightly beaten
Salt	$\frac{1}{2}$ tsp
Ground black pepper	$\frac{1}{4}$ tsp
Gelatine powder	15 g ($\frac{1}{2}$ oz), dissolved in 4 Tbsp hot chicken stock

Method

- Line a large colander with a piece of muslin cloth and place over a large mixing bowl. Set aside.

- Pour chicken stock and tomato juice into a large saucepan and stir in tomato purée, sugar, egg shell, egg white, salt and pepper. Bring mixture to the boil over high heat, whisking constantly.

- Remove from heat and stir in dissolved gelatine. Strain mixture through a colander several times or until liquid is completely clear.

- Pour mixture into a decorative mould and set aside to cool. When mixture has cooled completely, cover and refrigerate for at least 2 hours or until aspic has set completely.

- To unmould aspic, dip the base of mould into hot water, then place a chilled serving dish over mould and invert aspic onto dish. Gently ease aspic out of mould.

- Serve aspic on its own or as part of a salad.

tomato soufflés

An attractive and unusual dish that may be served as a light meal or an appetiser.

Makes 6 or 12

Ingredients

Tomatoes	6, large, or 12, medium
Butter	2 Tbsp
Plain (all-purpose) flour	30 g (1 oz)
Double (heavy) cream	2 Tbsp
Grated Parmesan cheese	2 Tbsp
Grated nutmeg	1/4 tsp
Dry mustard	1/2 tsp
Salt	1 tsp
Ground black pepper	1/2 tsp
Egg yolks	4
Egg whites	5

Method

- Preheat oven to 220°C (425°F).

- Slice caps off tomatoes and discard caps. Scoop out pulp and seeds and place in a pan. Set tomatoes aside. Place pan over low heat and simmer for 3 minutes. Remove from heat and strain tomato pulp through a fine wire mesh strainer. Discard dry pulp.

- In a small saucepan, melt butter over medium heat. Remove from heat and with a wooden spoon, stir in flour to make a smooth paste. Gradually add strained tomato mixture and cream, stirring constantly. Return pan to stove and and stir for 2 minutes over low heat.

- Add cheese, nutmeg, mustard, salt and pepper and stir to mix well. Remove from heat and leave to cool for 5 minutes.

- Stir egg yolks into tomato mixture, one at a time, beating until well blended. In a separate bowl, whisk egg whites until stiff peaks form. Using a metal spoon, fold egg whites into mixture until just combined.

- Pat insides of tomato shells dry with kitchen paper. Spoon in egg mixture until almost full, then place on a baking tray. Bake for 5 minutes, then lower temperature to 200°C (400°F) and continue to bake for another 15–20 minutes, or until tomato soufflés are golden brown on top.

- Carefully transfer tomatoes to a serving dish, garnish as desired and serve immediately.

tomato and chilli salsa

This zesty salsa is a great accompaniment to meat or fish dishes. Use within 4 hours of preparation as it does not keep well.

Serves 8

Ingredients

Firm tomatoes	4, peeled
Red onion	1, large, peeled and finely diced
Green capsicum (bell pepper)	1, cored, seeded and finely diced
Red chillies	2–3, seeded and finely chopped
Chopped coriander leaves (cilantro)	2 Tbsp
Red wine vinegar	90 ml (3 fl oz / $^3/_8$ cup)
Salt	$^1/_2$ tsp

Method

- Cut a small 'x' at the bottom of each tomato. Bring a pot of water to the boil and place tomatoes in for 30 seconds. Remove and plunge them immediately into cold water for another 30 seconds, then remove and drain. Peel and discard skins, then finely dice tomatoes.

- Place tomatoes and remaining ingredients in a china, glass or non-metallic bowl and mix well. Cover bowl and leave aside at room temperature for 30 minutes.

- Serve immediately as a side dish with meat or fish.

parmesan and sun-dried tomato scones

The combination of sun-dried tomatoes and cheese lend these scones a savoury twist, making them a tasty tea-time snack. Serve with unsalted butter if desired.

Makes 12

Ingredients

Water	125 ml (4 fl oz / ½ cup)
Sun-dried tomatoes in oil	2, drained and chopped
Plain (all-purpose) flour	220 g (8 oz)
Parmesan cheese	55 g (2 oz), grated
Sugar	2 Tbsp
Baking powder	1 tsp
Dried oregano	¾ tsp
Baking soda	½ tsp
Salt	½ tsp
Plain yoghurt	180 ml (6 fl oz / ¾ cup)
Olive oil	2 Tbsp
Egg whites	2

Method

- Bring water to the boil, then remove from heat. Add sun-dried tomatoes and set aside to soak for 30 minutes. Drain.

- Preheat oven to 200°C (400°F). Grease a baking tray lightly with some butter and set aside.

- Sift flour into a mixing bowl and add cheese, sugar, baking powder, oregano, baking soda and salt. Stir to combine and set aside.

- In a separate mixing bowl, combine sun-dried tomatoes, yoghurt, oil and egg whites. Mix well, then add to flour mixture and mix until just combined.

- Place dough on a lightly floured work surface. Dust hands with flour and knead lightly with your fingertips, until dough is smooth. Form dough into a 20-cm (8-in) circle and place on prepared baking tray. Without cutting through dough completely, make 6 shallow cuts to get 12 wedges.

- Bake for 15–20 minutes, or until surface of scone is light golden brown. Remove from heat and set aside to cool.

- Serve warm.

green tomato cake

The green tomatoes lend an natural sweetness to this cake, which has a moist yet light texture.

Makes one 22.5-cm (9-in) square cake

Ingredients

Green tomatoes	350 g (12 oz), chopped
Salt	1 Tbsp + a pinch
Butter	55 g (2 oz)
Castor (superfine) sugar	150 g (5$\frac{1}{3}$ oz)
Egg	1
Plain (all-purpose) flour	150 g (5$\frac{1}{3}$ oz)
Ground cinnamon	$\frac{1}{2}$ tsp
Ground nutmeg	$\frac{1}{2}$ tsp
Baking soda	$\frac{1}{4}$ tsp
Raisins	$\frac{1}{4}$ cup
Walnuts	$\frac{1}{4}$ cup, chopped

Method

- Place tomatoes in a bowl and sprinkle in 1 Tbsp salt. Leave aside for 10 minutes. Rinse tomatoes in cold water and set aside to drain in a colander until use.

- Preheat oven to 180°C (350°F). Line a 22.5-cm (9-in) square baking tin and set aside.

- In a mixing bowl, beat butter and sugar together until light and fluffy. Add egg and mix until just combined.

- Sift flour, cinnamon, nutmeg, baking soda and a pinch of salt into a separate mixing bowl. Add raisins and walnuts and mix well. Gradually fold flour mixture into butter mixture to form a stiff batter.

- Add tomatoes to batter and mix well. Do not overmix. Pour into prepared baking tin. Bake for 40 minutes or until top of cake is golden brown. Cake is done when a toothpick inserted into centre of cake comes out clean. Remove from heat and leave to cool slightly before removing from tin.

- Slice and serve warm.

dried cherry tomato muffins

Dried cherry tomatoes give these muffins a sweet taste and chewy texture.

Makes 12

Ingredients

Plain (all-purpose) flour	250 g (9 oz)
Sugar	100 g (3$\frac{1}{2}$ oz)
Baking powder	2 tsp
Sodium bicarbonate	$\frac{1}{4}$ tsp
Salt	$\frac{1}{4}$ tsp
Dried cherry tomatoes	55 g (2 oz)
Walnuts	30 g (1 oz), chopped
Milk	250 ml (8 fl oz / 1 cup)
Butter	125 g (4$\frac{1}{2}$ oz)
Egg	1, slightly beaten

Method

• Preheat oven to 190°C (370°F). Line a 12-hole muffin tin with paper cases.

• Sift flour, sugar, baking powder, sodium bicarbonate and salt into a mixing bowl and mix well. Stir in tomatoes and walnuts and set aside.

• In a mixing bowl, combine milk , butter and egg. Add to flour mixture and mix until just combined. Do not overmix.

• Spoon mixture into prepared muffin tin, filling cups two-thirds full. Bake for 20–25 minutes, or until muffin tops are golden brown.

• Remove from oven and leave aside to cool slightly on a wire rack. Serve warm.

sun-dried tomato, tofu and cheese muffins

Chewy and moist due to the use of silken tofu in place of flour, these muffins are great for vegetarians and those who are gluten-intolerant.

Makes 9 muffins

Ingredients

Silken tofu	200 g (7 oz), drained and mashed
Parmesan cheese	85 g (3 oz), grated
Cake flour	30 g (1 oz)
Almonds	140 g (5 oz), very finely ground
Baking powder	1 tsp
Sun-dried tomatoes in oil	1/4 cup, drained and finely chopped
Basil leaves	a handful, finely chopped
Water	4 Tbsp
Eggs	4, lightly beaten
Salt	1/2 tsp

Method

- Preheat oven to 200°C (400°F). Line a 9-hole muffin pan with paper cases.
- In a mixing bowl, place all ingredients and mix lightly until just combined. Do not overmix.
- Spoon mixture into prepared muffin pan and top with remaining Parmesan cheese. Bake for 30–35 minutes, or until tops are golden brown.
- Serve muffins warm or at room temperature.

tomato granita

Commonly served between courses to cleanse the palate, this savoury and slightly fiery granita will also perk up the taste buds!

Makes 8–10 servings

Ingredients

Ripe tomatoes	700 g (1½ lb)
Coriander leaves (cilantro)	2 sprigs
Lime juice	3 Tbsp
Tabasco sauce	1 Tbsp
Salt	to taste

Method

- Cut a small 'x' at the bottom of each tomato. Bring a pot of water to the boil and place tomatoes in for 30 seconds. Remove and plunge them immediately into cold water for another 30 seconds, then remove and drain. Peel and discard skins. Cut tomatoes in half. Scoop out and discard soft centres.

- In a blender, combine tomatoes, coriander, lime juice and Tabasco sauce and blend until smooth. Season with salt and stir to mix well.

- Transfer mixture to a shallow freezer container and freeze for about 1 hour, or until mixture has set around the edges.

- Using a fork, scrape to break up the ice crystals, then return to the freezer. Repeat at 30-minute intervals for 2–3 hours.

- Spoon shavings into serving glasses and serve between courses as a palate cleanser.

vegetables & salads

tomato pie

This tasty and filling pie makes an ideal meal for vegetarians, and goes well with a green salad.

Serves 4–6

Ingredients

Butter	1 tsp
Frozen shortcrust pastry	350 g (12 oz), thawed at room temperature
Tomatoes	450 g (1 lb), thinly sliced
Onion	1, medium, peeled and thinly sliced into rings
Button mushrooms	110 g (4 oz), caps wiped and coarsely chopped
Salt	1 tsp
Ground black pepper	$\frac{1}{2}$ tsp
Dried oregano	1 tsp
Dry mustard	1 tsp
Cheddar cheese	110 g (4 oz), grated
Egg	1, lightly beaten

Method

• Preheat oven to 190°C (370°F). Lightly grease a 22.5-cm (9-in) pie plate with butter and set aside.

• On a lightly floured work surface, roll out half of pastry into a 25-cm (10-in) circle. Line pie plate with dough and press down with your fingertips. Trim off excess dough and reserve trimmings.

• Place half of tomatoes, onion and mushrooms in the centre of the plate, leaving rim clear. Layer over half of salt, pepper, oregano, mustard and cheese. Continue layering until all ingredients are used up. Dampen edges of dough with water and set aside.

• Roll out remaining dough into a 25-cm (10-in) circle. Place over filling and press edges together. Trim off excess dough and reserve trimmings. Seal pie by crimping edges together.

• Roll out trimmings and cut into decorative shapes if desired and arrange on top of pie. Brush dough with beaten egg and cut a small cross at the centre for steam to escape.

• Place pie plate on a baking tray and bake for 30–40 minutes, or until pastry is golden brown and crisp. Remove from heat and leave aside to cool slightly.

• Serve immediately.

capsicum and tomato stew

Known in Italy as Peperonanta, this Italian stew of red capsicums and tomatoes can be enjoyed both hot and cold. Serve with a meat dish or as a light vegetarian meal.

Serves 4–6

Ingredients

Tomatoes	450 g (1 lb)
Butter	2 Tbsp
Olive oil	2 Tbsp
Onion	1, large, peeled and thinly sliced
Garlic	1 clove, peeled and crushed
Red capsicums (bell peppers)	450 g (1 lb), cored, seeded and cut into strips
Salt	$\frac{1}{2}$ tsp
Ground black pepper	$\frac{1}{4}$ tsp
Bay leaf	1
Fresh or dried rosemary leaves	for garnishing

Method

- Cut a small 'x' at the bottom of each tomato. Bring a pot of water to the boil and place tomatoes in for 30 seconds. Remove and plunge them immediately into cold water for another 30 seconds, then remove and drain. Peel and discard skins. Chop tomatoes and set aside.

- In a large saucepan, heat butter and oil over medium heat. When foam subsides, add onion and garlic and fry for 5–7 minutes, or until onion is soft and translucent but not brown.

- Add capsicums and cover pan. Reduce heat to low and leave to cook for 15 minutes. Add tomatoes, salt, pepper and bay leaf and simmer, uncovered, for 20 minutes, stirring occasionally. Mixture should be thick, with a moderate amount of liquid. Remove from heat and discard bay leaf.

- Dish out and serve immediately, garnished with rosemary leaves.

ratatouille

A classic French vegetable casserole with tomatoes as a key ingredient, ratatouille can be served as a main dish with steamed rice, or as an accompaniment to meat or fish.

Serves 4–6

Ingredients

Butter	1 Tbsp
Olive oil	4 Tbsp
Onions	2, large, peeled and thinly sliced
Garlic	2 cloves, peeled and crushed
Aubergines (eggplants/ brinjals)	3, medium, thinly sliced
Green and red capsicums (bell peppers)	1 each, cored, seeded and chopped
Courgettes (zucchinis)	5, medium, trimmed and sliced
Canned peeled tomatoes	390 g (14 oz), reserve juices from can
Dried basil	1 tsp
Dried rosemary	1 tsp
Salt	$1\frac{1}{2}$ tsp
Ground black pepper	$\frac{3}{4}$ tsp

Method

- In a large ovenproof casserole, heat butter and oil over medium heat. When foam subsides, add onions and garlic and fry for 5–7 minutes, or until onions are soft and translucent but not brown.

- Add aubergines, capsicums and courgettes and fry for another 5 minutes. Add tomatoes and reserved juices from can, basil, rosemary, salt and pepper and stir to mix well.

- Increase to high heat and bring mixture to the boil. Reduce heat to low, cover casserole and simmer for 40–45 minutes, or until vegetables are tender.

- Dish out and serve immediately.

NOTE

The cooking time specified in this recipe leaves the vegetables tender while retaining their shape. To have them softer, cook for another 15–20 minutes, stirring occasionally.

stewed fresh tomatoes

Use top-quality fresh tomatoes, as they are firm and full of flavour. This dish should be served as part of a Western meal.

Serves 4

Ingredients

Tomatoes	450 g (1 lb)
Butter	1 Tbsp
Oilve oil	1¹/₂ tsp
Spring onion (scallion)	1, finely chopped
Tomato purée	1 Tbsp
Garlic	1 clove, peeled and finely chopped
Sugar	¹/₂ tsp
Salt	to taste
Ground black pepper	to taste

Method

- Cut a small 'x' at the bottom of each tomato. Bring a pot of water to the boil and place tomatoes in for 30 seconds. Remove and plunge them immediately into cold water for another 30 seconds, then remove and drain. Peel and discard skins. Cut tomatoes into quarters. Set aside.

- In a frying pan, heat butter and oil over medium heat. When foam subsides, add spring onion and stir-fry for 1 minute. Stir in tomato purée until well mixed.

- Add garlic and tomatoes. Sprinkle in sugar, then season with salt and pepper to taste. Leave mixture to simmer for 2 minutes, tossing gently with a spatula.

- Dish out and serve immediately.

stuffed aubergines

Stuffed aubergines are a typical Mediterranean dish. Baking them ensures that they are cooked to tender perfection, without the greasiness of frying.

Serves 6

Ingredients

Tomatoes	350 g (12 oz)
Round aubergines (eggplants/ brinjals)	6, medium
Salt	
Olive oil	200 ml (6$\frac{1}{2}$ fl oz)
Onion	1, large, peeled and chopped
Garlic	3 cloves, peeled and crushed
Tomato purée	2 Tbsp
Ground allspice	1 tsp
Paprika	1 tsp
Chopped fresh parsley	2 Tbsp

Method

• Cut a small 'x' at the bottom of each tomato. Bring a pot of water to the boil and place tomatoes in for 30 seconds. Remove and plunge them immediately into cold water for another 30 seconds, then remove and drain. Peel and discard skins, then scoop out and discard soft centres. Chop tomatoes finely and set aside.

• Make 3 cuts lengthwise through each aubergine, leaving stem ends intact. Sprinkle exposed flesh with salt and leave to drain in a colander for 30 minutes.

• Meanwhile, heat 3 Tbsp olive oil in a pan over medium heat. Fry garlic and onions until onions are soft and translucent. Add tomatoes, tomato purée and spices. Reduce heat to low and leave mixture to simmer for 5 minutes. Remove from heat and add parsley. Rinse aubergines and pat dry with kitchen paper. Stuff slits with tomato mixture.

• Preheat oven to 200°C (400°F).

• Place aubergines in an ovenproof dish with cut side facing upwards. Pour remaining olive oil over and add enough boiling water to cover base of dish. Bake for 1 hour, or until aubergines are tender.

• Remove from heat and leave aside to cool. Refrigerate until chilled before serving.

sun-dried tomato dip

This tasty dip is great for serving at parties, accompanied with crackers or carrot and celery sticks. It can be prepared in advance and refrigerated until needed.

Serves 6–8

Ingredients

Sun-dried tomatoes in oil	2 Tbsp, drained and chopped
Cream cheese	110 g (4 oz)
Sour cream	55 g (2 oz)
Mayonnaise	1 Tbsp
Garlic	1 clove, peeled and minced
Tabasco sauce	1 tsp, or to taste
Salt	$\frac{1}{4}$ tsp
Freshly ground black pepper	$\frac{1}{4}$ tsp
Basil	5 leaves, chopped

Method

- Combine all ingredients in a blender and blend until smooth.
- Transfer dip to a serving bowl, cover and refrigerate until chilled.
- Serve with crackers or carrot and celery sticks.

courgette and tomato quiche

A delicately flavoured and colourful dish, this quiche can be enjoyed both hot and cold. Serve with a well-chilled white wine.

Makes one 22.5-cm (9-in) flan

Ingredients

Frozen shortcrust pastry	1 sheet, thawed at room temperature
Butter	55 g (2 oz)
Garlic	2 cloves, peeled and crushed
Courgettes (zucchinis)	4, trimmed and sliced
Salt	1 tsp
Ground black pepper	1 tsp
Dried oregano	$1/2$ tsp
Single (light) cream	125 ml (4 fl oz / $1/2$ cup)
Eggs	3
Cheddar cheese	55 g (2 oz), grated
Tomatoes	5, small, blanched, peeled and thinly sliced

Method

- Preheat oven to 190°C (370°F).

- On a lightly floured work surface, roll out pastry to fit a 22.5-cm (9-in) flan tin. Place some dried beans or baking weights on top of dough and bake for 15 minutes or until golden brown. Remove from heat and remove beans or baking weights. Set aside to cool. Increase oven temperature to 200°C (400°F) and keep warm.

- In a pan, melt butter over medium heat. When foam subsides, add garlic and fry for 1 minute or until fragrant. Add courgettes, $1/2$ tsp salt and $1/2$ tsp pepper and fry for 8–10 minutes, or until courgettes are lightly browned. Remove from heat and add remaining salt, pepper and oregano. Stir to mix well and set aside.

- In a mixing bowl, beat together cream, eggs and cheese until well mixed. Set aside.

- Arrange courgettes and tomato slices on top of pastry and pour cream mixture over. Bake for 35–40 minutes, or until filling is set and golden brown on top.

- Remove from heat and serve immediately, if serving hot.

tomato curry

This vegetarian Indian curry goes well with plain rice.

Serves 4

Ingredients

Tomatoes	900 g (2 lb), or use 800 g (1³/₄ lb oz) canned peeled tomatoes
Vegetable oil	85 ml (2¹/₂ fl oz)
Onions	2, medium, peeled and chopped
Ginger	5-cm (2-in) knob, peeled and finely chopped
Garlic	2 cloves, peeled and crushed
Green chillies	2, finely chopped
Ground turmeric	1 tsp
Ground coriander	2 tsp
Chilli powder	1¹/₂ tsp
Paprika	2 tsp
Plain yoghurt	3 Tbsp
Salt	1¹/₂ tsp
Sugar	1 tsp
Baby potatoes	450 g (1 lb), scrubbed

Method

- If using fresh tomatoes, cut a small 'x' at the bottom of each tomato. Bring a pot of water to the boil and place tomatoes in for 30 seconds. Remove and plunge them immediately into cold water for another 30 seconds, then remove and drain. Peel and discard skins and chop tomatoes finely. Place in a blender and process into a purée. Set aside.

- If using canned tomatoes, place in a blender and process into a purée. Set aside.

- In a large, heavy-based saucepan, heat 3 Tbsp oil over medium heat. Add onions and fry for 8–10 minutes, or until onions are golden brown. Add ginger, garlic and chillies and fry for 3 minutes or until fragrant.

- Combine turmeric, coriander, ¹/₂ tsp chilli powder, paprika and yoghurt in a small bowl. Add mixture to pan and fry for 5 minutes, stirring to mix well. Add tomatoes, ¹/₂ tsp salt and sugar and return mixture to the boil. Reduce heat to low, cover and leave to simmer for 20 minutes.

- Meanwhile, combine remaining chilli powder and salt in a bowl. Add potatoes and toss to coat. Add more salt and chilli powder to taste if desired. In a frying pan, heat remaining oil over medium heat. Add potatoes and fry for 5 minutes, or until lightly browned.

- Add potatoes to simmering mixture and simmer for another 20 minutes or until potatoes are tender.

- Dish out and serve immediately. Garnish as desired.

tomato and french bean salad

The simple, clean flavours of tomatoes and French beans complement each other perfectly. This salad also goes well with cold meats.

Serves 6–8

Ingredients

Tomatoes	450 g (1 lb), thinly sliced
French beans	450 g (1 lb), blanched, drained and diagonally sliced into 5-cm (2-in) lengths

Dressing

White wine vinegar	3 Tbsp
Olive oil	6 Tbsp
Salt	1/4 tsp
Ground black pepper	1/4 tsp
Prepared mustard	1/2 tsp
Sugar	1/2 tsp
Garlic	1 clove, peeled and crushed

Method

- Prepare dressing. Combine ingredients in a screw-top jar and shake vigorously until well mixed. Set aside.
- Place tomatoes and beans in a large serving dish and pour dressing over. Toss well, then refrigerate for 30 minutes to chill before serving.

tomato salad

This simple but elegant dish goes well with warm, crusty bread and butter. Serve with chilled white wine as an accompaniment to a poultry dish.

Serves 4

Ingredients

Firm tomatoes	450 g (1 lb), thinly sliced
Chopped spring onions (scallions)	1 Tbsp
Fresh basil leaves	a handful, thinly sliced

Dressing

Olive oil	3 Tbsp
White wine vinegar	1 Tbsp
Lemon juice	$\frac{1}{2}$ tsp
Prepared French mustard	$\frac{1}{4}$ tsp
Salt	$\frac{1}{2}$ tsp
Freshly ground black pepper	$\frac{1}{2}$ tsp

Method

- Prepare dressing. Combine all ingredients in a mixing bowl and beat with a fork until well blended.
- Arrange tomato slices in a serving dish and sprinkle spring onions over. Drizzle dressing over and garnish with basil leaves. Serve immediately.

sun-dried tomato loaf

Served with cold meats and a glass of red wine, this sun-dried tomato loaf brings home the flavours of the Mediterranean.

Makes I large loaf

Ingredients

Strong white bread flour	700 g (1$\frac{1}{2}$ lb)
Instant yeast	7 g ($\frac{1}{4}$ oz)
Pumpkin seeds	55 g (2 oz)
grated Parmesan cheese	85 g (3 oz) + 1 Tbsp
Warm water	435 ml (14 fl oz / 1$\frac{3}{4}$ cups)
Olive oil	3 Tbsp
Tapenade or black or green olive paste	6 tsp
Sun-dried tomatoes in oil	30 g (1 oz), drained

Method

- Sift flour into a mixing bowl. Add yeast, salt, pumpkin seeds and 85 g (3 oz) cheese and stir to mix well. Pour in warm water and olive oil and mix until a stiff dough is formed. On a lightly floured surface, knead dough for 10 minutes.

- Divide dough into 4 equal portions. Roll out into 20-cm (8-in) rounds. Spread 3 rounds with 2 tsp tapenade or olive paste each.

- Cut sun-dried tomatoes into large pieces and place on top of tapenade. Stack dough rounds with tapenade on top of each other. Roll out remaining dough round to a size big enough to enclose other layers. Place sheet on top of stacked dough and stretch to enclose other layers.

- Preheat oven to 200°C (400°F).

- Place dough on a baking tray and sprinkle with remaining cheese. Leave to proof for 30 minutes.

- Bake for 40 minutes, then reduce temperature to 180°C (350°F) and bake for another 10 minutes or until bread is golden brown. Leave aside to cool before serving.

NOTE

Tapenade is a paste made from puréeing olive flesh, garlic, capers and anchovies. Ready-made tapenade is available from some gourmet supermarkets. Alternatively, use black or green olive paste which is more widely available.

meat & poultry

steamed minced pork with tomatoes

This filling, nutritious dish is full of flavour due to the natural juices that exude from steaming the pork and tomatoes. Serve with rice.

Serves 4

Ingredients

Lean minced pork	300 g (11 oz)
Tomatoes	2, thinly sliced in rounds
Spring onion (scallion)	1, chopped
Salt	$1/2$ tsp
Cooking oil	2 tsp
Water	1 Tbsp
Ground white pepper	to taste

Method

- Place meat into a deep heatproof dish. Press lightly into a 1-cm ($1/2$-in) thick patty.
- Arrange tomato slices on top of meat and sprinkle spring onion over.
- Sprinkle salt and drizzle oil and water over meat. Season with pepper to taste.
- Place dish in a steamer and steam for 25–35 minutes, or until meat is well cooked.
- Serve immediately with plain white rice.

spicy tomato meatballs

Deliciously tangy, these meatballs are great paired with rice or pasta, and will be a hit among both children and adults.

Serves 4–5

Ingredients

Olive oil	4 Tbsp
Onions	2, peeled and finely chopped
Garlic	2 cloves, peeled and crushed
Tomatoes	450 g (1 lb)
Tomato purée	2 Tbsp
Sugar	1 tsp
Coriander seeds	1 Tbsp, crushed

Meatballs

Minced beef	450 g (1 lb)
Minced pork	250 g (9 oz)
Sliced white bread	2.5-cm (1-in) thick, crusts removed, soaked in cold water, then squeezed dry
Egg	1, large, lightly beaten
Salt	to taste
Ground black pepper	to taste

Method

- In a saucepan, heat 2 Tbsp oil over medium heat. Add onions and garlic and fry for 10 minutes, or until onions are soft and lightly browned. Add tomatoes, tomato purée, sugar and coriander seeds and stir to mix well. Reduce heat to low, cover and leave to simmer for 20–25 minutes, stirring occasionally. Remove from heat and set aside.

- Prepare meatballs. In a mixing bowl, combine ingredients, then shape into 20 meatballs.

- In a large frying pan, heat remaining oil over medium heat. Fry meatballs for 5–8 minutes, turning frequently until evenly browned. Drain excess oil, then add tomato mixture and stir to mix well. Reduce heat to low, cover and simmer for 30 minutes, stirring occasionally. Taste and adjust seasoning with salt and pepper if necessary.

- Dish out and serve hot.

NOTE

Meatballs can be kept for up to 6 months in the freezer. After cooking, leave to cool completely, then pour into a freezer container and freeze.

ladies fingers with tomatoes and bacon

A simple but hearty dish that can be enjoyed with rice or potatoes.

Serves 4

Ingredients

Plum (Roma) tomatoes	3
Bacon	2 slices
Onion	1, large, peeled and coarsely chopped
Ladies fingers	300 g (10^1/$_2$ oz), cut into 1-cm (^{1}/$_2$-in) lengths
Red chilli	1, seeded and sliced
Salt	to taste
Ground black pepper	to taste

Method

- Cut a small 'x' at the bottom of each tomato. Bring a pot of water to the boil and place tomatoes in for 30 seconds. Remove and plunge them immediately into cold water for another 30 seconds, then remove and drain. Peel and discard skins, then chop tomatoes and set aside.

- Heat a frying pan over medium to high heat. Fry bacon until brown and crisp. Drain and reserve drippings in pan. Cut bacon into small squares and set aside.

- In the same frying pan, fry onion in bacon drippings over medium heat until soft. Add tomatoes and fry for 1 minute, then add ladies fingers, chilli and bacon.

- Season with salt and pepper, then add just enough water to cover ingredients. Reduce heat to low, cover and leave to simmer for 30 minutes, or until ladies fingers are tender.

- Dish out and garnish as desired. Serve immediately.

pork chops with mushrooms and tomatoes

A succulent and simple dish to prepare, these pork chops go well with roast potatoes.

Serves 4

Ingredients

Boned pork loin chops	4, each about 1.5-cm ($^3/_4$-in) thick
Vegetable oil	2 Tbsp
Dried thyme	1 tsp
Salt	1 tsp
Ground black pepper	$^1/_2$ tsp
Butter	1 Tbsp
White button mushrooms	110 g (4 oz), caps wiped and sliced
Canned peeled tomatoes	390 g (14 oz), chopped, reserve juices from can
Dried sage	1 tsp
Chopped fresh parsley	1 Tbsp

Method

- Preheat grill to high. Arrange pork chops on a rack in a grill pan. Brush lightly with oil, then sprinkle with thyme, ½ tsp salt and $^1/_4$ tsp pepper.

- Grill pork chops for 5 minutes or faster on each side, then reduce heat to moderately low and grill for 15–20 minutes on each side, until thoroughly cooked and tender.

- Meanwhile, melt butter in a frying pan over medium heat. When foam subsides, add mushrooms and fry for 3 minutes. Add tomatoes with reserved juices, sage, parsley and remaining salt and pepper and stir to mix well. Reduce heat to low, cover and leave to simmer for 25 minutes, stirring occasionally.

- Place pork chops on a serving dish. Spoon tomato and mushroom sauce over and serve immediately.

beef stew

This hearty, warming stew is the perfect meal to consume on chilly nights. Serve with a tossed green salad, crusty bread and some red wine.

Serves 4

Ingredients

Stewing beef	900 g (2 lb), cut into 5-cm (2-in) cubes
Butter	55 g (2 oz)
Salt	1 tsp
Ground black pepper	½ tsp
Dried rosemary	½ tsp
Carrots	3, medium, peeled and cut into chunks
Turnip	1, small, peeled and cut into chunks
Onions	2, small, peeled
Potatoes	3, medium, peeled and halved
Canned peeled tomatoes	390 g (14 oz), reserve juices from can
Tomato purée	3 Tbsp

Marinade

Red wine	375 ml (12 fl oz / 1½ cups)
Beef stock	250 ml (8 fl oz / 1 cup)
Olive oil	3 Tbsp
Onion	1, large, peeled and thinly sliced
Black peppercorns	8
Garlic	3 cloves, peeled and crushed
Chopped fresh parsley	2 Tbsp
Dried rosemary	1 tsp
Bouquet garni	1, consisting of 4 sprigs parsley, 1 spray thyme and 1 bay leaf, tied together

Method

- Prepare marinade. In a large, shallow dish, combine ingredients for marinade and mix well. Place beef cubes in and leave to marinate in the refrigerator for 1–2 hours or longer if possible. Remove beef and pat dry with paper towels. Reserve marinade.

- In a large saucepan or pot, melt butter over medium heat. When foam subsides, add beef cubes and fry for 8 minutes, or until beef cubes are lightly and evenly browned.

- Add reserved marinade, salt, pepper and rosemary and stir to mix well. Increase heat and bring mixture to the boil. Skim off any scum that rises to the surface. Reduce heat to low, cover and leave to simmer for 1½ hours.

- Add carrots, turnip, onions, potatoes, tomatoes and reserved juices and tomato purée and stir to mix well. Replace cover and leave to simmer for 1 hour, or until meat is fork-tender. Remove and discard bouquet garni.

- Dish out and serve immediately.

osso buco

This classic Italian dish consists of veal shank or knuckle that is simmered in a rich gravy of tomatoes and wine, with the addition of gremolada for extra zest.

Serves 6

Ingredients

Seasoned flour	85 g (3 oz), made with 85 g (3 oz) plain (all-purpose) flour, 1 tsp salt and ½ tsp black pepper
Veal knuckle or shank	1.3 kg (3 lb), cut into 8-cm (3-in) lengths
Butter	110 g (4 oz)
Onion	1, large, peeled and thinly sliced
Canned peeled tomatoes	390 g (14 oz), reserve juice from can
Tomato purée	2 Tbsp
Dry white wine	180 ml (6 fl oz / ¾ cup)
Salt	1 tsp
Ground black pepper	½ tsp
Sugar	1 tsp

Gremolada

Finely grated lemon zest	1 Tbsp
Garlic	2 cloves, peeled and crushed
Finely chopped fresh basil	1½ Tbsp

Method

- Place seasoned flour on a large plate. Roll veal pieces in flour and coat well. Shake off excess flour and set aside.

- In a large saucepan or pot, melt butter over medium heat. When foam subsides, add veal pieces and fry for 5–8 minutes, or until lightly and evenly browned. Remove veal with a slotted spoon and place on a plate. Set aside.

- In the same saucepan or pot, add onion and fry for 5–7 minutes, or until soft and translucent but not brown. Add tomatoes with reserved juice from can and tomato purée and stir to mix well. Cook for 3 minutes.

- Pour in wine and sprinkle in salt, pepper and sugar. Increase heat and bring mixture to the boil. Return veal to the saucepan or pot and stir to mix well. Reduce heat to low, cover and leave to simmer for 1½–2 hours, or until veal is fork-tender.

- Meanwhile, prepare gremolada. In a small mixing bowl, combine ingredients and mix well. Add gremolada to saucepan or pot and leave to simmer for another 1 minute.

- Transfer veal to a serving dish. Ladle gravy over and serve immediately.

tomato chicken omelette

This easy-to-prepare dish can be served as a light meal or quick snack.

Serves 2

Ingredients

Olive oil	1 Tbsp
Butter	2 Tbsp
Shallots	2, peeled and finely chopped
Garlic	1 clove, peeled and crushed
Tomatoes	2, small, blanched, peeled, seeded and chopped
Minced chicken	100 g (3$\frac{1}{2}$ oz)
Chopped fresh parsley	1 tsp
Chopped fresh tarragon	1 tsp, or $\frac{1}{4}$ tsp dried tarragon
Eggs	4
Salt	$\frac{1}{4}$ tsp
Ground black pepper	$\frac{1}{2}$ tsp
Cold water	1$\frac{1}{2}$ Tbsp

Method

- Heat oil and melt half of butter in a frying pan over medium heat. When foam subsides, add shallots and garlic and fry for 3–4 minutes, or until shallots are soft and translucent but not brown.

- Add tomatoes and chicken and fry for 3 minutes, or until chicken changes colour and is cooked. Add parsley and tarragon and stir to mix well. Remove from heat and set aside. Keep warm.

- In a mixing bowl, beat eggs, salt, pepper and cold water together with a fork until well mixed. Divide egg mixture into 2 equal portions and set aside.

- In a clean frying pan, melt $\frac{1}{2}$ Tbsp remaining butter over medium heat. When foam subsides, add 1 portion of egg mixture to cook an omelette. Remove to a serving plate. Repeat for remaining portion of egg mixture.

- Spoon chicken and tomato filling equally onto omelettes, then fold omelettes over into semi-circles.

- Garnish as desired and serve immediately.

mozzarella chicken

A delicious combination of tomatoes and melted cheese drizzled over tenderly grilled chicken breast.

Serves 6

Ingredients

Vegetable oil	2 Tbsp
Onion	1, medium, peeled and finely chopped
Canned peeled tomatoes	390 g (14 oz), reserve juices from can
Tomato purée	2 Tbsp
Dried oregano	1 tsp
Salt	1 tsp
Ground black pepper	$\frac{1}{2}$ tsp
Streaky bacon	6 slices, rinds removed
Butter	2 Tbsp
Finely chopped fresh tarragon	1 tsp, or $\frac{1}{4}$ tsp dried tarragon
Chicken breasts	6, skinned and boned
Mozzarella cheese	110 g (4 oz), sliced

Method

- In a saucepan, heat oil over medium heat. Add onion and fry for 5–7 minutes, or until soft and translucent but not brown.

- Add tomatoes with reserved juices, tomato purée, oregano, salt and pepper and stir to mix well. Increase heat and bring to the boil. Reduce to very low heat and leave to simmer for 20 minutes, stirring occasionally. Remove from heat and set aside.

- Meanwhile, heat a frying pan over high heat and fry bacon until brown and crisp. Drain and reserve drippings in pan. Leave bacon to drain on absorbent paper. Keep warm.

- Add butter to the same pan and melt over medium heat. When foam subsides, add tarragon and chicken and fry for 15–20 minutes, or until chicken is tender and cooked. Do this in batches if necessary.

- Preheat grill to high.

- Transfer chicken to a heatproof serving dish and place a slice of bacon over each breast. Spoon tomato sauce over and place cheese on top. Grill for 4–5 minutes, or until cheese has melted and is light brown.

- Remove from heat and serve immediately.

tomato and chicken salad

This refreshing salad, flavoured with fresh tarragon, chives and garlic, makes an ideal light meal.

Serves 4

Ingredients

Chicken breast	450 g (1 lb), cooked and diced
Tomatoes	450 g (1 lb), sliced
Hard-boiled eggs	4, peeled and sliced
Bacon	4 rashers, rinds removed, grilled until crisp and chopped
Avocado	1, large, halved, stoned, peeled and sliced

Dressing

Garlic	2 cloves, peeled and crushed
Chopped fresh tarragon	1½ Tbsp, or 1 Tbsp dried tarragon
Finely chopped fresh chives	1 Tbsp
Salt	1¼ tsp
Ground black pepper	¾ tsp
Lemon juice	2 tsp
Sour cream	3 Tbsp
Mayonnaise	125 ml (4 fl oz / ½ cup)

Method

- Prepare dressing. Combine all ingredients for dressing in a salad bowl and mix well. Add salad ingredients and toss gently until ingredients are well coated with dressing.
- Refrigerate for at least 30 minutes to chill before serving.
- Garnish as desired.

roasted tomato fondue

These roasted kebabs are delicious when dipped in the rich tomato dip.

Makes 16 kebabs

Ingredients

Bacon	8 rashers, rinds removed
Red cherry tomatoes	8
Yellow cherry tomatoes	8
Long aubergine (eggplant/ brinjal)	1, cut into 16 chunky pieces
Onions	2, peeled and each cut into 8 pieces
Cooking oil	2 Tbsp

Tomato Dip

Roma (plum) tomatoes	450 g (1 lb), halved
Olive oil	2–3 Tbsp
Basil leaves	2–3 sprigs, torn
Garlic	2 cloves, peeled and thinly sliced
Salt	to taste
Freshly ground black pepper	to taste

Method

- Preheat oven to 200°C (400°F).

- Prepare dip. Place tomatoes, cut side up, on a roasting tray. Drizzle olive oil over and sprinkle with basil leaves and garlic. Season with salt and pepper. Roast for 20–25 minutes, or until tomatoes are soft, with their juices running. Remove and discard basil leaves. Transfer tomatoes and roasting juices to a blender and blend until smooth. Pour into a serving bowl and set aside. Keep warm.

- Cut each bacon rasher in half, lengthwise and roll up. Thread a rolled up bacon rasher through a skewer, alternating with cherry tomatoes, aubergine pieces and onions. Make 16 kebabs in total.

- In a grill pan, heat oil over medium heat. Grill kebabs for 3–5 minutes, turning once.

- Serve kebabs immediately, with tomato dip on the side.

calzones

Serve this piping hot, for a superb snack or main course, with a fresh green salad.

Serves 4

Ingredients

Olive oil	2 Tbsp
Onion	1, peeled and chopped
Garlic	2 cloves, peeled and crushed
Canned chopped tomatoes	800 g (1¾ lb)
Chopped fresh oregano	1 Tbsp
Salt	to taste
Ground black pepper	to taste
Chilli powder	½ tsp
Pepperoni	110 g (4 oz), thinly sliced
Mozzarella cheese	225 g (8 oz), diced

Dough

Strong plain flour	450 g (1 lb)
Salt	1 tsp
Instant yeast	7 g (¼ oz)
Warm water	275 ml (9 fl oz)
Olive oil	4 Tbsp

Method

- In a saucepan, heat oil over medium heat. Add onion and garlic and fry over medium heat for 5 minutes, or until onions are soft. Add tomatoes, oregano, salt and pepper and stir to mix well. Bring mixture to the boil, then reduce heat to low and simmer, uncovered, for 1 hour, or until sauce has reduced and thickened. Remove from heat and leave aside to cool.

- Preheat oven to 220°C (440°F).

- Sift flour into a mixing bowl. Add salt and yeast and stir to mix well. Pour in warm water and olive oil and mix until a stiff dough is formed. On a lightly floured surface, knead dough for 10 minutes until smooth.

- Divide dough into 4 equal portions. Roll out and use a 22.5-cm (9-in) round cutter to cut dough into circles.

- Add chilli powder, pepperoni and cheese to cooled tomato sauce and stir to mix well. Spoon 2–3 Tbsp sauce onto one half of each dough circle and spread with the back of a spoon, leaving edges untouched.

- Dampen edges of dough by dabbing with a little water. Fold ends of dough circles together to enclose filling and crimp edges to seal.

- Place calzones on a lightly greased baking tray. Lightly brush surface with water and bake for 20 minutes, or until calzones are well-risen, firm and golden brown.

- Serve hot.

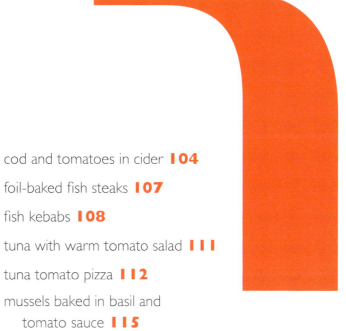

fish & seafood

cod and tomatoes in cider

This simple dish does not take long to prepare and is versatile enough to be served either with potatoes, crusty bread or rice.

Serves 4

Ingredients

Tomatoes	350 g (12 oz)
Butter	30 g (1 oz)
Cod steaks	4, each about 200 g (7 oz), skinned
Dry cider	150 ml (5 fl oz / 10 Tbsp)
Salt	to taste
Freshly ground black pepper	to taste
Chopped fresh parsley	2 Tbsp
Chopped fresh thyme	1 Tbsp, or 2 Tbsp dried thyme

Method

- Preheat oven to 200°C (400°F).

- Cut 1 tomato into 4 rounds and set aside. Place remaining tomatoes in a large basin of hot water. Cover bowl and leave aside for 1 minute. Drain tomatoes, then peel and discard skins. Chop finely and set aside.

- Using a little butter, lightly grease a shallow ovenproof dish. Add chopped tomatoes, then place cod steaks on top.

- In a saucepan melt remaining butter over low heat. When foam subsides, add cider and stir to mix well. Remove from heat and pour over cod. Season with salt and pepper, then sprinkle parsley and thyme over. Place tomato rounds on top of cod.

- Bake for 20 minutes, or until cod is thoroughly cooked. Serve immediately.

NOTE

Dry cider is an alcoholic cider that contains between 5 and 7 per cent alcohol. It is not sweet, as the natural sugar has been fermented out. If unavailable, apple cider may be used, but the dish will taste sweeter and not have as much 'bite' to it.

foil-baked fish steaks

Baking fish in foil packets helps retain flavour and moistness. Use fish with firm, white flesh such as cod or snapper.

Serves 4

Ingredients

Olive oil	3 Tbsp
Butter	90 g (3 oz)
Green capsicum (bell pepper)	1, large, cored, seeded and finely chopped
Celery	1 stalk, chopped
Onion	1, large, peeled and finely chopped
Tomato ketchup	200 ml (6$\frac{1}{2}$ fl oz)
Garlic	2 cloves, peeled and finely chopped
Salt	to taste
Ground white pepper	to taste
Firm-fleshed white fish steaks	4, each about 180 g (6$\frac{1}{2}$ oz)

Method

- Preheat oven to 190°C (370°F).

- Heat oil and melt half the butter in a frying pan over medium heat. When foam subsides, add capsicum, celery and onion and fry until onion is soft and translucent but not brown.

- Add tomato ketchup and garlic, then season with salt and pepper to taste. Stir to mix well, then leave to simmer gently for 10 minutes, stirring occasionally. Remove from heat and set aside.

- Pat fish steaks dry with kitchen paper and season lightly with a little salt and pepper. Heat remaining butter in another pan over medium heat. Add fish and fry until golden brown on both sides.

- Cut 4 sheets of aluminium foil large enough to wrap each fish completely. Spread 2–3 Tbsp tomato mixture in the centre of each foil sheet. Place a fish steak on top and spread 1 Tbsp tomato mixture over. Wrap fish completely and fold edges to seal securely.

- Place fish parcels on a baking tray and bake for 10–15 minutes, or until fish is thoroughly cooked but still firm.

- Serve immediately.

fish kebabs

These kebabs offer a great way to serve fish, while showing off the potential of grilled tomatoes.

Makes 4

Ingredients

Firm white fish	700 g (1½ lb), skinned and deboned, cut into 3-cm (1½-in) cubes
Cherry tomatoes	16
Button mushrooms	220 g (8 oz), caps wiped
Green capsicum (bell pepper)	1, cored and seeded, cut into 2.5-cm (1-in) squares
Dry white wine	125 ml (4 fl oz / ½ cup)
Olive oil	3 Tbsp
Salt	½ tsp
Paprika	½ tsp
Lemon	1, cut into quarters

Method

• Thread fish cubes on 4 long metal skewers, alternating them with tomatoes, mushrooms and capsicum squares. Set aside.

• In a large shallow dish, combine wine, olive oil, salt and paprika. Lay skewers in dish and leave to marinate at room temperature for 2 hours, turning occasionally.

• Preheat grill to high.

• Place kebabs on grilling rack and grill for for 5–7 minutes, turning frequently, or until fish flakes easily when tested with a fork.

• Remove kebabs from heat. Add a wedge of lemon to the end of each skewer and serve immediately.

tuna with warm tomato salad

A warm salad dressing and pine nuts go perfectly with this simple, Mediterranean-style dish.

Serves 4

Ingredients

Tuna steaks	4, each about 175 g (6 oz) and 1.2-cm ($\frac{1}{2}$-in) thick
Lime	1, juice extracted
Olive oil	5 Tbsp + extra for greasing
Pine nuts	55 g (2 oz)
Red pesto	1 Tbsp
Red wine vinegar	1 Tbsp
Soft dark brown sugar	a pinch
Tomatoes	450 g (1 lb), thinly sliced
Lime	1, cut into wedges

Method

- Preheat grill to high.

- Place tuna steaks in a shallow non-metallic dish. Combine lime juice and 2 Tbsp oil, then spoon over tuna. Cover and leave to marinate in the refrigerator for 30 minutes, turning steaks over once. Reserve marinade.

- Lightly grease a grilling rack with oil and place tuna steak on top. Grill for 8–10 minutes on each side, or until tuna flakes easily when tested with a fork. Baste both sides of tuna steaks with marinade every few minutes while grilling. Remove from heat and set aside.

- Heat remaining oil in a frying pan over medium heat. Add pine nuts and fry for 1 minute, or until golden brown, stirring frequently. Remove from heat and leave to drain on absorbent paper.

- Using the same pan, combine red pesto, vinegar and sugar over low heat. Stir until sugar dissolves completely, then remove from heat.

- Arrange tomato slices on a serving plate. Pour vinegar and sugar mixture over tomatoes and sprinkle with pine nuts. Season with pepper to taste.

- Place tuna steaks on prepared serving plate, being careful not to break fish. Serve immediately with lime wedges on the side.

tuna tomato pizza

Made with a scone base, this pizza is topped with cheese and canned tuna flakes and makes a delicious lunch or light snack.

Makes one 25-cm (10-in) pizza

Ingredients

Pastry

Butter	2 Tbsp + 1 tsp
Self-raising flour	220 g (8 oz)
Baking powder	1 tsp
Salt	$^1/_2$ tsp
Freshly ground black pepper	$^1/_4$ tsp
Dried basil	$^1/_4$ tsp
Dried oregano	$^1/_4$ tsp
Cheddar cheese	55 g (2 oz), grated
Milk	160 ml (5 fl oz / $^5/_8$ cup)

Topping

Canned tuna chunks	200 g (7 oz), drained and flaked
Canned peeled tomatoes	390 g (14 oz), drained and sliced
Dried oregano	$^1/_2$ tsp
Salt	$^1/_4$ tsp
Ground black pepper	$^1/_4$ tsp
Cheddar cheese	220 g (8 oz), grated

Method

- Preheat oven to 220°C (440°F). Lightly grease a baking tray with 1 tsp butter and set aside.
- Sift flour, baking powder, salt and pepper into a large mixing bowl. Add basil and oregano and stir to mix well. Using your fingertips, rub 2 Tbsp butter into flour until mixture resembles coarse breadcrumbs. Add cheese and enough milk to form a soft dough.
- On a lightly floured work surface, roll dough out into a 25-cm (10-in) circle. Place on prepared baking tray.
- Top dough with tuna flakes, then tomato slices. Sprinkle oregano, salt, pepper and cheese over and bake for 30–35 minutes, or until cheese has melted and pastry is cooked through.
- Remove from oven and transfer pizza to a serving dish. Slice and serve immediately.

mussels baked in basil and tomato sauce

Enjoy this delicious dish of mussels in a rich tomato gravy on its own as a one-dish meal.

Serves 4

Ingredients

Fresh mussels	1.8 kg (4 lb), soaked for 30 minutes in salted water, or 560 g (1¼ lb) canned mussels, drained
Butter	1 Tbsp + 1 tsp
Olive oil	3 Tbsp
Onion	1, large, peeled and finely chopped
Garlic	3 cloves, peeled and crushed
Canned peeled tomatoes	700 g (1½ lb), chopped, reserve juices from can
Salt	½ tsp
Ground black pepper	¼ tsp
Chopped fresh basil	3 Tbsp or 1½ Tbsp dried basil
Fresh breadcrumbs	2 Tbsp
Parmesan cheese	55 g (2 oz), grated

Method

- If using fresh mussels, soak in a large basin of water for 30 minutes for them to expel any sand. Remove mussels from basin, being careful not to agitate sand at bottom of basin. Scrub mussels under running water.

- Place mussels in a steamer and steam gently for about 8 minutes, or until mussels open. Discard any that do not open. Remove mussels from shells and set aside. Discard shells.

- Preheat oven to 180°C (350°F). Lightly grease a baking dish with 1 tsp butter and set aside.

- Heat oil and melt remaining butter in a saucepan over medium heat. When foam subsides, add onion and garlic and fry for 5–7 minutes, or until onion is soft and translucent but not brown.

- Add tomatoes with reserved juices, salt, pepper and basil and stir to mix well. Reduce heat to low and leave to simmer for 15 minutes, stirring occasionally. Remove from heat and stir in steamed or canned mussels. Pour mixture into prepared baking dish.

- In a small mixing bowl, combine breadcrumbs and Parmesan cheese and mix well. Sprinkle over mussels and bake for 20 minutes, or until breadcrumb layer is golden brown. Remove from heat and serve immediately.

chilli crabs

Tangy and spicy, this seafood dish is popular in Singapore and Malaysia. Mop up excess gravy with deep-fried buns or plain white bread.

Serves 4

Ingredients

Mud crabs	2, large
Cooking oil	125 ml (4 fl oz / $\frac{1}{2}$ cup)
Garlic	4 cloves, peeled and finely chopped
Ginger	2.5-cm (1-in) knob, peeled and grated
Onions	2, peeled and finely chopped
Red bird's eye chillies	3, seeded and finely chopped
Tomato ketchup	125 ml (4 fl oz / $\frac{1}{2}$ cup)
Sweet chilli sauce	125 ml (4 fl oz / $\frac{1}{2}$ cup)
Sugar	2 Tbsp
Tamarind pulp	$\frac{1}{2}$ Tbsp, mixed with 1$\frac{1}{2}$ Tbsp warm water and strained
Light soy sauce	1 Tbsp
Egg	1, beaten

Method

- If crabs are alive, place in the freezer for a few hours. Remove and scrub crabs clean. Remove triangular flap on the underside of each crab, then pull top shell off. Remove gill filaments and rinse crabs. Cut crabs into 4 pieces, then remove pincers. Use a mallet to crack pincers. Set crabs aside.

- In a wok, heat oil over high heat. Add crabs and fry until shells turn red. Remove and set aside. Discard half the oil.

- Reheat oil over medium heat and add garlic, ginger, onions and chillies. Fry until onion is soft and garlic, ginger and chillies are fragrant, then stir in tomato ketchup, chilli sauce and sugar. Bring mixture to the boil, stirring occasionally.

- Return crabs to wok and cook for 10 minutes. Stir in tamarind liquid and soy sauce and return to the boil. Drizzle egg into wok so it does not form into clumps and remove to a serving dish. Egg will cook in the residual heat.

- Garnish as desired and serve immediately.

crab rösti cakes with tangy tomato corn salsa

Accompanied with a tangy tomato and corn salsa, these crab and potato cakes make a delicious treat!

Serves 4

Ingredients

Crab meat	180 g (6$\frac{1}{2}$ oz)
Potatoes	300 g (11 oz), peeled, grated and squeezed dry
Garlic	1 clove, peeled
Ginger	2.5-cm (1-in) knob, peeled
Salt	$\frac{1}{2}$ tsp
Spring onions (scallions)	3, chopped
Chilli powder	a pinch
Plain (all-purpose) flour	2 tsp
Egg	1, beaten
Vegetable oil	

Tomato Corn Salsa

Canned sweet corn kernels	180 g (6$\frac{1}{2}$ oz)
Garlic	1 clove, peeled and crushed
Plum (Roma) tomatoes	2, chopped
Spring onions (scallions)	4, chopped
Tomato purée	1 tsp
Lime	1, juice extracted
Chilli powder	a pinch
Salt	

Method

- Prepare salsa. Drain sweet corn and place in a bowl. Using the back of a spoon, crush kernels slightly, then add remaining ingredients and stir to mix well. Leave aside for 30 minutes to allow flavours to infuse.

- In a bowl, combine crab meat and potatoes. Using a mortar and pestle, pound together garlic, ginger and salt until pasty, then mix with crab meat mixture. Add spring onions, chilli powder and flour and mix well. Stir in egg.

- Fill a frying pan with oil until it reaches 1 cm ($\frac{1}{2}$ in) up the sides of pan. Heat oil over medium heat. Drop tablespoonfuls of mixture, about 4–5 at a time, into hot oil and cook for 5 minutes on each side, or until golden brown and potato is cooked. Remove and drain on absorbent paper. Repeat until crab meat mixture is used up.

- Serve hot with tomato corn salsa on the side.

tomato and prawn choux pastry ring

This savoury choux pastry ring is an adaptation of the classic French gourère.

Serves 6

Ingredients

Butter	30 g (1 oz)
Onion	1, medium, peeled and thinly sliced
Plain (all-purpose) flour	30 g (1 oz)
Chicken stock	125 ml (4 fl oz / $^1/_2$ cup)
Tomato chutney (page 35)	3 Tbsp
Tomatoes	3, large, blanched, peeled and chopped
Prawns (shrimps)	110 g (4 oz), peeled
Salt	$^1/_4$ tsp
Ground black pepper	$^1/_4$ tsp
Cheddar cheese	55 g (2 oz), grated

Choux Pastry

Water	250 ml (8 fl oz / 1 cup)
Butter	125 g ($4^1/_2$ oz)
Sugar	1 tsp
Plain (all-purpose) flour	150 g ($5^1/_3$ oz)
Eggs	4

Method

- Lightly grease a 30-cm (12-in) ovenproof flan dish with a little butter.

- Prepare choux pastry. In a large saucepan, bring water to the boil. Add butter and sugar, stirring continuously until butter has melted completely. Reduce heat to low and add in flour. Stir continuously until mixture is cooked and leaves sides of pan. Remove from heat.

- Beat in eggs one at a time, until well blended before adding the next. Mixture should be thick, smooth and shiny. Set aside.

- Preheat oven to 200°C (400°F).

- In a large saucepan, melt remaining butter over medium heat. When foam subsides, add onion fry for 5–7 minutes until onion is soft and translucent but not brown. Remove from heat. With a wooden spoon, stir in flour until a smooth paste is formed. Gradually add stock, stirring continuously.

- Return pan to the stove over medium heat, stirring constantly for 2–3 minutes, or until sauce is thick and smooth. Remove pan from heat and stir in chutney, tomatoes and prawns. Season with salt and pepper and set aside.

- Spoon choux pastry mixture in large mounds about 1-cm ($^1/_2$-in) apart, around edge of prepared flan dish. Spoon tomato and prawn mixture into centre of dish and sprinkle grated cheese over. Bake for 30–35 minutes, or until choux pastry has doubled in size and is light brown in colour.

- Pierce pastry with the point of a sharp knife to allow steam to escape. Serve immediately.

rice & pasta

tomato rice

This simple Indian rice dish is redolent with the fragrance of garlic and onion. Serve with chicken, lamb or meat curries.

Serves 6

Ingredients

Butter	3 Tbsp
Onions	2, medium, peeled and finely chopped
Garlic	1 clove, peeled and crushed
Ginger	2.5-cm (1-in)
Red capsicum (bell pepper)	1, cored, seeded and finely sliced
Canned peeled tomatoes	390 g (14 oz), finely chopped, reserve juice from can
Long-grain rice	350 g (12 oz), washed and soaked in cold water for 30 minutes and drained
Salt	1 tsp
Ground black pepper	$1/4$ tsp

Garnish

Spring onion (scallion)	1, thinly sliced

Method

- In a large saucepan, melt butter over medium heat. When foam subsides, add onions, garlic and ginger and fry for 5–7 minutes, or until onions are soft and translucent but not brown.

- Add capsicum and fry for another 3–5 minutes. Add chopped tomatoes with reserved juices and rice and stir to mix well. Add enough water to cover rice, then season with salt and pepper and bring mixture to the boil. Reduce heat to low, cover and simmer for 15–20 minutes, or until all the liquid is absorbed and rice is cooked and tender.

- Dish out, garnish with spring onion and serve immediately.

pork fried rice

This recipe offers a quick and convenient way to use up leftover rice.

Serves 4

Ingredients

Cooking oil	2 Tbsp
Garlic	2 cloves, peeled and crushed
Pork	300 g (11 oz), thinly sliced
Onion	1, peeled and finely diced
Tomato purée	3 Tbsp
Fish sauce	2 Tbsp
Cooked long-grain rice	700 g (1½ lb), chilled, preferably a day old
Ground white pepper	to taste

Method

- In a wok, heat oil over medium heat. Add garlic and fry until fragrant, then add pork and stir-fry for 2–3 minutes lightly until cooked.

- Add onion, tomato purée and fish sauce and stir to mix well. Add some water and oil if mixture becomes too dry.

- Increase to high heat and add rice. Use a spatula to break up any lumps in rice and mix well. Season with pepper and remove from heat.

- Dish out, garnish as desired and serve immediately.

arborio rice with pork

This Spanish dish makes a delicious one-dish meal and may be served with a fresh green salad for extra crunch.

Serves 4

Ingredients

Olive oil	2 Tbsp
Spanish onion	1, peeled and sliced
Garlic	2 cloves, peeled and crushed
Trimmed pork shoulder	900 g (2 lb), cut into 2.5-cm (1-in) cubes
Canned chopped tomatoes	390 g (14 oz)
Water	435 ml (14 fl oz / 1$\frac{3}{4}$ cups)
Arborio rice	175 g (6 oz)
Paprika	1 Tbsp
Green olives	110 g (4 oz), pitted

Method

- In a large saucepan, heat oil over medium heat. Add onion and fry for 5 minutes or until soft. Add garlic and fry for 1–2 minutes.

- Increase heat and add pork cubes. Fry for 8 minutes or until meat is evenly browned. Add tomatoes and water and stir to mix well. Bring to the boil, then reduce to low heat, cover and leave to simmer for 45 minutes, stirring occasionally.

- Add rice, paprika and olives and stir to mix well. Leave to simmer, uncovered, for another 30 minutes, or until almost all the liquid has been absorbed and rice is tender.

- Dish out and serve immediately.

NOTE

Arborio rice is a classic risotto rice from northern Italy. It may sometimes be labelled as risotto rice. The grains can absorb a large amount of liquid without becoming overly soft. When cooked, it should still have a slight bite to it.

lasagne

This baked pasta dish is homey and comforting. Savour with a glass of full-bodied red wine.

Serves 4

Ingredients

Olive oil	1 Tbsp
Butter	50 g (1⅔ oz)
Onion	1, peeled and chopped
Streaky bacon	4 slices, cut into strips
Lean minced beef	450 g (1 lb)
Lean minced pork	200 g (7 oz)
Canned tomatoes	390 g (14 oz)
Dry red wine	150 ml (5 fl oz / ¾ cup)
Tomato purée	2 Tbsp
Dried basil	½ tsp
Grated nutmeg	½ tsp
Salt	to taste
Ground black pepper	to taste
Plain (all-purpose) flour	50 g (1⅔ oz)
Milk	575 ml (19 fl oz)
Lasagne sheets	6–8
Mozzarella cheese	125 g (4½ oz), grated

Method

- Heat oil and melt half the butter in a large saucepan over medium heat. Add onion and fry for 5 minutes until soft. Add bacon and fry for 2–3 minutes, or until bacon is brown and crisp.

- Add minced beef and pork. Using a wooden spatula, break meat up and stir-fry for 3–5 minutes, or until meat is browned. Add tomatoes, wine, tomato purée, basil, nutmeg, and salt and pepper. Reduce to low heat and simmer, covered, for 30 minutes, stirring occasionally. Remove lid and increase heat to medium. Cook for another 20–30 minutes, or until sauce is reduced and thickened. Remove from heat and set aside.

- Heat oven to 220°C (425°F). Melt remaining butter in a small saucepan over low heat. Add flour and milk and stir to mix well. Cook for 3 minutes until mixture thickens. Bring mixture to the boil, reduce heat to low and leave to simmer for another 3 minutes, stirring constantly. Remove from heat and set aside.

- Pour half the meat and tomato sauce into a 1.25-litre (40-fl oz / 5-cups) gratin dish. Arrange a layer of lasagne sheets on top and pour just slightly less than half of flour and milk mixture over. Top with remaining meat and tomato sauce and another layer of lasagne sheets. Pour remaining white sauce over and sprinkle with grated Mozarella.

- Bake for 30–40 minutes, or until cheese is golden brown and pasta is cooked. Cover dish with foil and cook longer if necessary. Serve immediately.

seafood marinara

A treat for seafood lovers, this spicy tomato-based pasta dish makes a satisfying meal.

Serves 4

Ingredients

Clams	300 g (11 oz)
Spaghetti or linguini	300 g (11 oz)
Extra virgin olive oil	1 Tbsp
Butter	30 g (1 oz)
Garlic	2 cloves, peeled and finely chopped
Onion	1, large, peeled and finely copped
Bird's eye chilli	1, finely chopped
Canned peeled tomatoes	600 g (1 lb 5¹/₃ oz), chopped
Chopped parsley	2 Tbsp
White wine	250 ml (8 fl oz / 1 cup)
Lemon	1, grated for zest
Sugar	¹/₂ Tbsp
Prawns (shrimps)	600 g (1 lb 5¹/₃ oz), peeled and deveined
Scallops	200 g (7 oz), roe removed, rinsed, drained and halved
Salt	to taste
Ground black pepper	to taste

Method

- Soak clams in a large basin of water for 30 minutes for them to expel any sand. Remove from basin, being careful not to agitate sand at bottom of basin. Scrub clams under running water, then drain and set aside.

- Bring a pot of salted water to the boil. When water is boiling, add spaghetti or linguini and cook until al dente. Drain and keep warm.

- In a frying pan, heat oil and butter over medium heat. When foam subsides, add garlic, onion and chilli and fry until fragrant and onion is soft.

- Add tomatoes, parsley and wine and stir to mix well. Bring to the boil and leave to simmer, uncovered, for 8–10 minutes, or until sauce has reduced and thickened slightly.

- Add lemon zest, sugar, prawns, scallops and clams. Cover and leave to simmer for 5–7 minutes, or until clams open. Discard any that do not open. Season with salt and pepper and remove from heat.

- Spoon sauce over pasta and toss to mix well. Serve immediately.

ravioli with tomato sauce

Although it takes a longer time to prepare, this tomato-based Italian dish is worth all the effort. It is generally served as a first course, but can also be enjoyed as a main dish for lunch or dinner.

Serves 6

Ingredients

Store-bought fresh meat and spinach ravioli	600 g (1 lb 5$\frac{1}{3}$ oz)

Tomato Sauce

Olive oil	2 Tbsp
Onion	1, small, peeled and finely chopped
Tomatoes	900 g (2 lb), blanched, peeled, seeded and chopped
Canned peeled Italian tomatoes	390 g (14 oz), reserve juices from can
Tomato purée	70 g (2$\frac{1}{2}$ oz)
Dried basil	$\frac{1}{2}$ tsp
Dried oregano	$\frac{1}{2}$ tsp
Sugar	1 tsp
Salt	$\frac{1}{2}$ tsp
Ground black pepper	$\frac{1}{2}$ tsp

Garnish

Pecorino cheese	55 g (2 oz)
Chopped fresh parsley	1 Tbsp

Method

- Prepare tomato sauce. In a saucepan, heat oil over medium heat. Add onion and fry for 5–7 minutes, or until onion is soft and translucent but not brown.

- Add fresh and canned tomatoes, reserved juices, tomato purée, basil, oregano, sugar, salt and pepper and stir to mix well. Bring to the boil, then reduce heat to low, cover and leave to simmer for 40 minutes, or until sauce is thick. Remove from heat and set aside.

- Bring a pot of water to the boil. When water is boiling, add ravioli and cook until al dente. Remove, drain and place in an ovenproof casserole.

- Preheat grill to high.

- Pour tomato sauce over ravioli and sprinkle evenly with cheese. Grill for 5 minutes, or until cheese is melted and golden brown.

- Remove from heat and serve immediately.

spicy broccoli and sun-dried tomato pasta

This pasta dish can be enjoyed both hot or cold. Vary the greens used as desired. Asparagus are a good choice.

Serves 4

Ingredients

Fusilli	300 g (11 oz)
Olive oil	4 Tbsp
Chopped garlic	1 Tbsp
Broccoli	1 small head, cut into florets
Sun-dried tomatoes (dry)	3/4 cup, soaked in hot water to soften, then drain and diced
Lemon juice	2 tsp
Chilli flakes	to taste
Grated Parmesan cheese	to taste

Method

- Bring a pot of salted water to the boil. When water is boiling, add fusili and cook until al dente. Drain and keep warm.

- In a pan, heat oil over medium heat and fry garlic until light brown. Add broccoli and sun-dried tomatoes and stir to mix well. Reduce heat, cover and cook over low heat until broccoli is tender. Drizzle lemon juice over and add chilli flakes.

- Spoon broccoli mixture over pasta. Toss to mix well and sprinkle with Parmesan cheese.

- Serve immediately.

fettuccine with tuna and artichoke hearts in sun-dried tomato sauce

Sun-dried tomatoes have a sweet flavour and a lovely chewy texture, making them ideal in this chunky tomato-based sauce.

Serves 4

Ingredients

Fettuccine	300 g (11 oz)
Olive oil	2 Tbsp
Garlic	2 cloves, peeled and finely chopped
Onion	1, peeled and finely chopped
Fresh thyme	1 sprig, chopped
Dry white wine	4 Tbsp
Chicken stock	250 ml (8 fl oz / 1 cup)
Lemon juice	2 Tbsp
Lemon zest	1 tsp
Sun-dried tomatoes in oil	30 g (1 oz), drained and chopped
Canned artichoke hearts	55 g (2 oz), sliced
Canned tuna chunks	200 g (7 oz), drained
Salt	to taste
Freshly ground black pepper	to taste

Method

- Bring a pot of salted water to the boil. When water is boiling, add fettucine and cook until al dente. Drain and keep warm.

- In a large saucepan, heat oil over medium heat. Add garlic and onion and fry until onion is soft. Add thyme and stir to mix well. Fry for another 2 minutes, or until onion is golden brown.

- Add white wine and leave to cook until only 3 Tbsp liquid is left. Add chicken stock, lemon juice and lemon zest. Reduce heat and leave to simmer for 10 minutes, or until liquid has reduced by about one-third.

- Add sun-dried tomatoes, artichoke hearts and tuna and stir to mix well. Cook just until heated through.

- Spoon artichoke and sun-dried tomato mixture over fettucine and toss to mix well. Season with salt and pepper.

- Serve immediately.

glossary

1. Arborio rice

Arborio grains are slightly roundish in shape and of medium length. Primarily used to make risotto, an Italian rice dish, the grains have a high starch content that produces a creamy texture when cooked.

2. Aubergines (eggplants/brinjals)

There are many varieties of aubergines, from short and round, to long and thin. Cultivars grown in Asia tend to be smaller and more slender as compared to Western cultivars. Due to their mild, neutral taste and spongy texture, they absorb other flavours well during cooking. Choose aubergines that have smooth, unblemished skin.

3. Canned peeled tomatoes

Canned tomatoes are a good substitute when fresh tomatoes are not available. They can be used to make chunky pasta sauces as well as the base sauce for pizzas. Choose tomatoes that are packed in juices rather than purée, as they tend to have a "fresher" taste.

4. Celery salt

Essentially a mixture of ground celery seeds and salt, celery salt is used as a seasoning ingredient.

5. Chilli powder

Chilli powder is made from grinding dried chillies into a fine powder. Depending on the type of chilli it is made from, chilli powder varies in its level of spiciness. It should be stored in a cool, dark place away from moisture.

6. Dried cherry tomatoes

Dried cherry tomatoes retain much of their original flavour, with an added dimension of sweetness. Whether freeze-dried, sun-dried or oven-dried, dried cherry tomatoes should have an intense dark red colour and a dry, pliable texture.

7. Dried tarragon

Dried tarragon is a good substitute when fresh leaves are not available. The greyish green leaves have a subtle, sweet flavour that is reminiscent of anise or liquorice, and go well with chicken and fish dishes.

8. Green tomatoes

Green tomatoes are essentially unripe tomatoes. Tart, with a slightly acidic flavour, they have a crunchy texture and tend to be firmer than their ripe counterparts. Green tomatoes hold up well when they are breaded and fried, or made into pickles and chutney.

9. Ladies fingers

Also known as okra, ladies finger is a native African vegetable that is now widely available all over the world. Shaped like a long, slender pod, its body is ridged and covered with fine hairs. When cooked, ladies fingers release a sticky substance that acts as a thickener.

10. Paprika

Made from ground dried capsicums (bell peppers), paprika adds a subtle spiciness to dishes. It may vary in spiciness and colour, depending on the capsicums used.

11. Pecorino cheese

Made from sheep's milk, the Italian name "pecorino" denotes fresh, medium-aged and mature forms of the cheese. Depending on its age, pecorino cheese ranges in its flavour and colour. Fresh pecorino cheese is soft and mild-tasting, whereas a mature cheese is firmer and saltier.

12. Pine nuts

Pine nuts have a sweet, soft texture. They are usually roasted before use, and add an extra crunch and flavour to salads, pastas and meat dishes. Pine nuts are widely available packed in plastic, and should be used as quickly as possible upon opening.

13. Pumpkin seeds

Flat and green in colour, pumpkin seeds have a sweet, nutty flavour. They can be used in salads, breads and pastries to add an added dimension of texture and flavour, or eaten on their own as a snack.

14. Red and yellow cherry tomatoes

Small and sweet, cherry tomatoes are typically used in salads and can also be consumed on their own as a snack. Like their bigger cousins, cherry tomatoes have various cultivars that vary in texture, shape, size and taste.

15. Tomato juice

When freshly squeezed and chilled, tomato juice makes a refreshing beverage that contains all of the vitamins and antioxidants of a fresh tomato. It is also used as a base ingredient for cocktail drinks, such as Bloody Mary.

16. Tomato purée

Tomato purée is usually available in cans or tubes. It is usually made from Roma (plum) tomatoes or any cultivar of tomato that has a firm, juicy constitution, and may vary in its texture. Tomato purée can be used to make pasta sauces or added to soups and stews.

Weights and Measures

Quantities for this book are given in Metric, Imperial and American (spoon and cup) measures. Standard spoon and cup measurements used are: 1 tsp = 5 ml, 1 Tbsp = 15 ml, 1 cup = 250 ml. All measures are level unless otherwise stated.

Liquid And Volume Measures

Metric	Imperial	American
5 ml	1/6 fl oz	1 teaspoon
10 ml	1/3 fl oz	1 dessertspoon
15 ml	1/2 fl oz	1 tablespoon
60 ml	2 fl oz	1/4 cup (4 tablespoons)
85 ml	2 1/2 fl oz	1/3 cup
90 ml	3 fl oz	3/8 cup (6 tablespoons)
125 ml	4 fl oz	1/2 cup
180 ml	6 fl oz	3/4 cup
250 ml	8 fl oz	1 cup
300 ml	10 fl oz (1/2 pint)	1 1/4 cups
375 ml	12 fl oz	1 1/2 cups
435 ml	14 fl oz	1 3/4 cups
500 ml	16 fl oz	2 cups
625 ml	20 fl oz (1 pint)	2 1/2 cups
750 ml	24 fl oz (1 1/5 pints)	3 cups
1 litre	32 fl oz (1 3/5 pints)	4 cups
1.25 litres	40 fl oz (2 pints)	5 cups
1.5 litres	48 fl oz (2 2/5 pints)	6 cups
2.5 litres	80 fl oz (4 pints)	10 cups

Dry Measures

Metric	Imperial
30 grams	1 ounce
45 grams	1 1/2 ounces
55 grams	2 ounces
70 grams	2 1/2 ounces
85 grams	3 ounces
100 grams	3 1/2 ounces
110 grams	4 ounces
125 grams	4 1/2 ounces
140 grams	5 ounces
280 grams	10 ounces
450 grams	16 ounces (1 pound)
500 grams	1 pound, 1 1/2 ounces
700 grams	1 1/2 pounds
800 grams	1 3/4 pounds
1 kilogram	2 pounds, 3 ounces
1.5 kilograms	3 pounds, 4 1/2 ounces
2 kilograms	4 pounds, 6 ounces

Oven Temperature

	°C	°F	Gas Regulo
Very slow	120	250	1
Slow	150	300	2
Moderately slow	160	325	3
Moderate	180	350	4
Moderately hot	190/200	375/400	5/6
Hot	210/220	410/425	6/7
Very hot	230	450	8
Super hot	250/290	475/550	9/10

Length

Metric	Imperial
0.5 cm	1/4 inch
1 cm	1/2 inch
1.5 cm	3/4 inch
2.5 cm	1 inch

Abbreviation

tsp	teaspoon
Tbsp	tablespoon
g	gram
kg	kilogram
ml	millilitre

Lincolnshire
COUNTY COUNCIL

tomatoes